A CHANGE OF MAPS

A CHANGE *of* MAPS

poems by

Carolyne Wright

For Katherine,
Wonderful to meet you "under
the lowering, perfect sky,
back in the Pacific Northwest
We'll continue
our
conversations!

LOST HORSE PRESS
Sandpoint · Idaho

Abrazos,
Carolyne

16 September 2006

Book design by Christine Holbert
Author photo by Ann Borden

FIRST EDITION

Library of Congress Cataloging-in-Publication Data

Wright, Carolyne, 1949-
A change of maps : poems / by Carolyne Wright.—1st ed.
    p. cm.
ISBN-13: 978-0-9762114-3-3 [alk. paper]
I. Title.
PS3573.R498C47 2006
811'.54—dc22

                              2005037302

Books of Poetry

Stealing the Children
Premonitions of an Uneasy Guest
Seasons of Mangoes and Brainfire

Chapbooks

Returning What We Owed
From a White Woman's Journal
Brief Irreveries
Greatest Hits: 1975-2001

Translations

In Order to Talk with the Dead: Selected Poems of Jorge Teillier
(from the Spanish)

The Game in Reverse: Poems by Taslima Nasrin
(from the Bengali)

Another Spring, Darkness: Selected Poems of Anuradha Mahapatra
(from the Bengali)

Majestic Nights: Love Poems by Bengali Women

Nonfiction

A Choice of Fidelities: Lectures and Readings from a Writer's Life

TABLE OF CONTENTS

A Change of Maps

The Custody of the Eyes

In memory of my father, Maurice C. Wright,
and of my mother, Marian Lee Wright

—For Jim, my compass's True North

 ## A CHANGE OF MAPS

"Thus should have been our travels . . ."

—*Elizabeth Bishop*

STUDIES WITH MISS BISHOP

"... awful but cheerful."
—*from "The Bight"*

A small, stumpy woman with frumpy, silvered coiffure
and a scarf of pure froth floating at the throat of her

Bonwit Teller suit (linen, I think, in powdered lilac pearl), she raised
basilisk-lidded grey eyes to the dazed

clutch of undergraduates clustered in the same Parrington Hall
classroom where Roethke had blazed and blustered in mythic, maniacal

dolor—that afternoon of pencils and paper-clips and fine pale
dust filtering Gauloises she smoked to muster her own pedagogical

energies. Her opening words abashed and stunned us,
eager neophytes, Walt and Emily wannabes, poesy's poseurs.

"First of all, I don't like teaching, but the trust
fund ran out—exhausted—so we'll make the best

go of it we can. You'll write in form,
good practice even if you never manage a real poem

here." Practice we did: sonnets, sestinas, villanelles—
heroic measures, hexameters' long vowels

improvised in our contrary Anglo-Saxon stresses
in syllables that tripped our tongues and stumbled as

jots and dashes ... Ashes she spilled—when I dropped a name: *Rio de
Janeiro*—down her *crêpe de chine* blouse. "Do you

know Brasil?" she asked me in her office. I was awed. I
knew that *"the Bishops spoke only to the Lowells, and the*

Lowells only to God." In wishful syllables, my
lingering Portuguese, I relived Brasil's Ash Wednesday

melancholy, riding from Bahia to Mutum, *monte adentro,*
Minas Gerais and its rain-ragged hills, green as sorrow.

"Not the easiest country to love," she sighed. Then,
"not the easiest country to abandon.

Only a fond fool," she said, "would settle in Ouro Prêto."
Or (she didn't say) *a woman in love with Lota's shadow.*

Pages turned, we never spoke of her Brasilians,
poets who unlearned love's evanescent lessons.

Questions we students were never bold enough to ask: her
quixotic absences from class, she declined to deliver

Roethke's Memorial Reading at her residency's close,
resonance of bourbon in asthmatic metaphors.

So much I didn't know that distracted season—
she staggered past me, unseeing, one April afternoon

toward campus, clumsy in her Minnie Mouse black shoes,
timid wind twisting through the Sitka spruce

under which she stopped to gasp, her breath rasping in
uncanny panic. How did she recover, masking in

vertiginous dignity her retreat? I didn't dare
venture from cover, volunteer my arm. I watched her

wend back up the street . . . and on to Harvard, NYU,
Wesleyan . . . and the dropped telephone at Lewis Wharf. No

xeroxed handouts from our classes, from those years before
xerography, survive. So how, friends ask, can you assure

you worked with her? Where's your first-read contract with *The New
Yorker?* My evidence? a life's uneasy parallels: a new

zip code every year, no tenure, child, or lover going spousal. Still,
Zen's empty bowl runneth over. Awful? Yes! But cheerful!

LOVE AFFAIR IN A SMALL TOWN

That was the winter we clung to each other
in a bed that obeyed too well
the laws of gravity, in an apartment
big enough for someone who was always out.
It was Anywhere, USA, and always snowing,
like those Norman Rockwell cards that urged us
to put the Christ back in Christmas.
We X'd ourselves out of the landscape.
How else to silence the tales
boots tell, in a town that had words

only for denial? We were each other's
best-kept secret, as snow drowned out
the traffic, and neighbors trudged by,
scanning mailboxes for names to match
the lights in upstairs windows.
What did we have to hide?
Our old lovers at opposite ends
of the continent, we answered
the telephone as easily as the couple
who sheltered a family

of illegal aliens for years. We
took turns sleeping,
pinning notes to the refrigerator
like a calendar of private references.
You played songs from the days
we believed music had the answers,
and I worked over my books till dawn.
Mornings, you slipped into the chair
behind me, hands under my sweater,
the toy airplane you gave me

doing spins and backflips
on the table. We moved toward
each other as if dreaming the receding
last words of a song. We didn't need
anyone to forgive us for what
we learned—ache of your tongue in my mouth,
the flush under our skin lingering
for hours, love a skill
we were in no hurry to tire of.
We who would never give

ourselves away, in a season
where no one else could have saved us.
We wanted, we said, nothing else.
A wind between two seasons,
our real lives miles away inside us.
We weren't looking for other names
or numbers. As the old year
flooded the snowbanks with its on-again
off-again lights, you helped me pack
for a life I couldn't return to.

We never even asked *What next.*
Those last weeks, it seemed the town went on
forever, and we kept looking back
as if we could never leave, as if
we were already gone—losing ourselves
under the lowering, perfect sky.
Nothing could have made us
any more or any less than what
we were, and we had a whole continent
in which to change our minds.

A CHANGE OF MAPS

Early fall looks both ways
into the year—how we will outsmart
the distance. Behind us, our childhoods
wave goodbye in the rear-view mirror.

We look ahead, down avenues
of poplars whose buried pasts reflect
in limbs that take root in the water.
Where we are going: the X factor,

unguessed as the gaps between wavelengths.
Our maps: not the Triple A's
network of routes, its field guides
to speed traps and warm weather;

but navigation charts, parchment
rough as Magellan's reckoning.
Blank seas and *terrae incognitae*.
Coastlines wandering off in fanciful

directions, peninsulas bulging
wrongly as anatomically
impossible limbs. The mapmakers'
crabbed Latin can't explain

how such charts voyaged into the New World
of our luggage. Magic, we say,
armchair pilgrims, turning page
after page of color-coded nations,

asking no questions of our whereabouts.
Above us, satellites measure the drift
of continents, dissolving vows
of bedrock, offshore shelves conceding

all their striations to the sea.
They track the moon's loosening orbit,
explorer shuttles homing in
with batteries of data, micro-

chips shrinking our wildest dreams.
We roll up the old cartographies,
coordinates overlaid with newer,
more transparent certainties

in the subatomic shadows' glare.
Where now? we want to know of landscape—
houses and poplars and children the maps
and master planners have no idea of.

Our arrival will coincide with the true
colors of our going. We look
both ways for distances that shift
their bearings in our favor.

A REPLY TO STORMS IN NEW ORLEANS

—For my mother in Seattle

Nothing unholy about lightning where
I come from. No nightly pyrotechnics,
no Voudoun-Thor hurling his thunderbolts
upside the sky, great swags of rain-laurel
slapping the jalousies. Never the dull
pressing-down of cloud-cover, breezeways
in heat-stunned swelter, saltwater
glaze on the skin. Not the river
twelve feet above the city, the levee
that cradles the current in its arms
rolling slow as thunder. No monsoon's
straight-down drench, Creole sweetness
and *crepuscule* making an evening of afternoon.

Where I grew up, I never had to shun
standing under slash pines, never run
through the shotgun row of rooms
unplugging lamps and window fans.
I never had to lie down with a man
as far as bodies can from door frames
and let the tempest steal words from
our mouths. No silence before the storm
or drips from eaves like afterthoughts.

Where I'm from, storms poured out
their cumulus contents and moved on,
silver as parachute-silk linings.
For them, no barometric records
made to be broken, no sopped sponges
in the corners, no oleander shrubs
huddled on the neutral ground along Elysian

Fields, beaten flat by baseball hail.
I never skidded into wrong turns
down one-way canals of street-flood,
or flipped over in some impassable
cul-de-sac between Piety and Desire,
wheels spinning against grillework.

Only once, the postwar powerlines fallen,
my father across the Cascade rain front
in Spokane, thunder over Alki Point
gunning its engines on the roof,
my mother stuck candles in a loaf
of bread, the kitchen beyond the tapers
dim as a Rembrandt interior. My mother
younger than she'd ever be again.
It's the birthday party of the rain,
she said, to quiet my baby brother's whimper.

Nighthawks circle, crying for direction.
Sunsets here are late, Arctic.
Light lingers like an obsession,
a hand remembered on a shoulder.
Night trawlers cross the harbor,
holding out their lamps
at masts's length like old men
seeking someone who tells the truth.

Light lingers like an obsession,
the truth's conflicting claims.
Night trawlers cross the harbor,
holding out their lamps where
the headlands darken, like old men
who seek someone to simulate the moon.
In this Arctic wind, I am amazed
at the extraordinary courage of the trees.

Hands recall their bruising rhythms
that linger like multiple entendres
over the darkening bluffs. Why do I
talk around it? We go on living.
The brave trees creak in the wind,
wind that blows from the Sound
all day, all night across the harbor
like the truth's conflicting claims.

Voices collect in the solar wind,
lanterns over Arctic water simulate the moon
at apogee, questions we held at mast's length
to go on living. Air-ocean reverse
polarity, vicissitudes of wind

across headland and harbor, the hemlocks'
extraordinary courage. Our words circled
back on themselves with obsessive breaths

the way night trawlers cross the moon's wake
with question marks, lamps on shore
brighten with heartache's reckless precision.
"How high the moon?" we talked around ourselves
as air and ocean switched polarities
over the heart's unfinished country. The truth—
we hesitated, lost ourselves in lamplight
while nighthawks circled, crying for direction.

CLAMMING AT TAHUYA

Hood Canal, Washington

Low tide. The great blue herons fished,
      jabbing long heads into underwater weather,
           wading through silt shallows
on stick-figure stilts. Candlefish
      thrashed silver past harpoon points.
           Our boots broke into lives there,

barnacle flutings crimped as old lace,
      shells that chinked and clattered
           like antique shards. Once
we came upon a Gumboot chiton
      big as a shoe: dun-colored
           blob with a scratched and scumbled

carapace. A sci-fi film's alien
      invader tumbled through the ozone-
           layer blaze and battened on sand
of its new planet, it dared to plant
      its bulk against us.
           We trudged on,

but the sealed lips of oyster shells
      gave nothing away. Geoduck clams
           chunked like dropped clocks into
rusty buckets. How deeply the brine
      flats sighed, the razor clams' air holes
           bubbled, as our trespassers' weight

pressed tide-fill from our bootprints.
      A heron folded up the long splints
           of its legs, sailed out across the bay

on slow aeilerons, a fantasy contraption
        from the early days of flight.
                Iodine stains of kelp

spread to the neap line,
        silt crackled with flagella
                welcoming the rich sea home.
Guilty,
        the battered chiton at our feet said,
                its shape that reminded us of extinction.

We set buckets down, tried to put away
        the evidence: tide tables, trowels for
                thrusting in packed sand, penknives
for prying mussels open.
        The smell of greed, like kelp-tangle,
                unshakeable from our pockets.

THE ICE-CLIMBER

Upper Grindelwald Glacier

A single climber, making his way
handhold by handhold over the blue
labial folds of the glacier.

A man roped only to himself
under a sky closing down, breaking
the first rule of avalanche weather.
Never climb on ice alone.

"He's either crazy," you whispered,
"or extremely good."
Your broken climber's trepidation.
Who else would train
for the North Face of the Eiger?

Below him, the cave's mouth gaped,
its aquamarine walls shimmering
as if airbrushed
with a network of white veins.

                    The cavern
we thought we recognized: old
rotogravures, hikers from Zürich
and Lausanne, with their staffs
and Tyrolean leather, posed
on sand-littered steps cut into ice
that was inching forward even as they stood.

Where Goethe kept his famous balance
one fine October afternoon of 1779,
clambering onto the Stauchwall
of the latest slide, peasant women
in dirndls steadying the ladders, before
the glacier clock was invented.

We'd followed the climber's filling bootprints
from the lot at the road's end,
his battered Citröen already hands-deep
under spruce-bough-bending snow,

past the last chalets, past the red
"*Lawinen: Zugang verboten!*" warnings,
each sign brighter and more urgent
than the one before.

Early winter's sugar snow
pulled away from our boots
in loosening scrolls: a warming trend,
damp lassitude of the air.

We halted beside the refuge chalet,
with its dried-apple strands
and cordwood stacked under the eaves—
where his tracks dropped over
the lip of the slope, its sagging twine barrier
like a final caution,

down the glacier's lateral path.
We trained our binoculars
where upthrust ice buckled
like a sinking liner's prow
into the snow-drowned base of the moraine.

Below him, his cramp-ons had printed
a wavering trail, skirting fracture lines
between crevasses. Gill-like striations
of ice into which blue shadows vanished.

He set ice-screws into the scumbled face,
and clipped carabiners through the loops—
a flawed intention to belay himself
across the fissures.
Lilliputian tapping of his ice-axe
reached us an instant later
over the split-second chasm of sound.

Then a roar dawned deep in the slope.
Don't speak. Don't even breathe,
you hissed, as the slope itself

split off, slab ice and frost-fractured slate
poured down the glacier's corrugated channel
and divided on either side
of the outcropping to which he clung.

For a long while
silence: echoes' aftermath
like subliminal daybreak
muffled by the warming snow.

For a long while
silence: echoes' aftermath
like subliminal daybreak
muffled by the warming snow.

We left him on the glacier.
All the way down, we glanced back,
at every curve, on the plank bridge
where our steps rang false

over the Lütschine's cheap-green roil,
too cheerful a hue for what flows
from the eon's-deep grind of ice
down the mountain.

                            Alone
he unrolled himself, picked up his axe,
shouldered the belaying rope,
and went on. Trail of his cleatprints
slipping inch by inch behind him
in the creak of ice resuming its advance.

Who else on earth knew where he was?
Decades hovered in the air above him,
the sky sifting stellar crystals, sleet
in all its shifting temperatures.

CELEBRATION FOR THE COLD SNAP

Pre-dawn's pilot lights
glow under the burners
like the vigil lamps
of runways. Not one
but has kept the faith all night.

At six the window squares
go blue, the first commuter
trains clang by, full
of people with bills to pay, important
telephones to answer, custom-made
ornaments for their office tree.

She labors alone, draping tinsel
on her foot-high pine,
turning the world news
down to a simmer. She parses words
together, makes lists of things
she can do without: gifts
and their impossible demands.

Old lovers' faces rise and set
in her thoughts. Their hands
reach for her, toadstools
that spring up in one rain.
She glues their greeting cards
to the mirrors, the year's
discarded printouts.

She wraps presents to herself.
Free of the Big World
and its confusion of envies,
she stands at the window,

watches trains crawl past: everyone
she's had to let go of,
sleepwalkers lost in the heart's
subzero weather.

AFTER THE EXPLOSION OF MOUNT ST. HELENS, THE RETIRING GRADE-SCHOOL TEACHER GOES FOR A LONG WALK THROUGH THE WHEATLANDS

Odessa, Washington

These were the fields of the moon:
a dream of crops
and the distant cataclysm's
new snow ghosting on the roadway,
white as elevation markers
she could no longer point to on the wall maps.

All afternoon across the wheat steppes.
Hills mauve with slant-light, spring wheat
green-graying to the horizon.
She followed the straight track between the fields
on faith: no barns anywhere
to show her what arrival looked like.

No trees either . . . No, one—
over a rise, a poplar. Its gray leaves
drooped, dejected as a scolded child.
The geography she taught
told her *Hidden Springs.* Or *History*—
a farmhouse, torn down now, and a farmer

who planted a sapling once
thinking "avenue,"
and collapsed at the end
of a drought-cracked summer
before he ever could remember shade.

She kicked ash drift at the road's edge.
It rose heavily, reluctant
as eraser dust on the hands of blackboard
monitors she kept late after school.
The road went on, endless as an open set
as if whole numbers could extend
as far as sky does over the horizon.

Her last few weeks.
The ruler-straight road
reminded her who the teacher was.
She trudged between forty-acre sections,
chalk dust from the hundred sentences
deepened the lines of a neglected
history lesson in her face.

HISTORICAL SITE

"...the historical calm of a site
Where something was settled once and for all"
—*W.H. Auden*

Where something happened. The sequoia
that couldn't help itself for growing.
The pass between avalanches
miraculously there as a first blizzard
battered the timberline
and the warm dream of valleys
fell face forward in the settlers' tracks.
The rock face the ambush party had to climb
or not live to regret it. Events
extreme as love: once or forever,
not again.

Cars thread through the eye
in the General Sherman's trunk.
The pass is triple lanes each way,
no U-turns at the overlook.
Behind the parking lot, the Alpine
Properties home office, a green sign
points up the rock face, pink floodlights
improve upon it every night.

                              Nothing
of this ever meant to happen. Macadam
laid once, no going back. Love
foresworn, red tags on stakes
working up the mountain. We put money
down— a green root through basalt.
A marriage of convenience with the stone.

RETURN TO SEATTLE: BASTILLE DAY

No difference in the gray gulls, sobbing
like women who circled the tumbrels,
scaffold silhouettes of fir.
The same sky lowers over the channel,

the plane follows it down
like an obsession, guillotine blade
of sun on water. All of this
for what? Walking the green neighborhoods

with names like gracious women: Madrona,
Magnolia. Rain telling its stories
on the ponds, rainbows fracturing
in oil slicks. How could I go back

to where I first took my age
between my hands like a lover's face
and said, *"This far, no farther"*?
Then moved from one coastline

to the next, as if I had
no winter and no home? For years
it was easy: nothing to answer
for what went beyond the weather,

too soon to give up on the body
or lose myself in the blue
selectivity of dream.
Now, what stands between me

and the long frontier with winter—
A father, sleepwalking among ohms
and voltmeters, the electric smell
of metal. A brother, face-down

in the soft gray light
of the calculus. A sister,
vanished from the glass house
of her thoughts before anyone

could have grown into her name.
My mother, 1945, stepping from
the Armistice Day prop plane
with her unchanged face,

light off the Cascade rain front
troubling her memory with its danger,
years before she could blame
herself for everything.

BILDUNGSGEDICHT

At sixteen, I roamed Seattle Center with Johnny
Dee, the wicked-thin, mop-topped rock singer
who'd bopped into the Piccoli Theatre
while we rehearsed *Kind Lady*, and straightaway
asked me out. "Like, I dig your style,"

he drawled, lounging in a cracked plastic
chair under the Food Circus awning. Slipping
off his mirror shades, he talked of gigs
and record deals, his band "the hottest, you dig?,
in the whole South End." So, would I be his chick?

Hours later, he put me on the city bus
to View Ridge. "Ta, luv," he grinned. So cool.
So British. I waved to him through tinted windows
till he vanished in a swirling plume of diesel.
"Where have you been?" my mother fumed,

stabbing a toothpick into her midnight slice
of avocado. "Oh mother!" I rolled my eyes.
"Chill out! It was a long rehearsal." My senses
tuned to night, I waited for the phone to ring.
"Mom, do you like my hair like this?"

I poked at it in the mirror. "Hey Mom?
You think I can sing?" A week slid by. He showed
up at dress rehearsal, in a blue tailored
Beatles suit, with his sidekick Don, who played drum
and bass. "I dig your threads,"

he chuckled, tightening his arm around my gauzy
black frock, on the park bench by the fountain. Don
slouched, smoking, at the other end. "So foxy."
He kissed me, and took a cigarette from Don.
"Hey, you're gonna dig this song

I wrote for you." His tenor was smoky and nasal
like Dylan's in *A Hard Rain's Gonna Fall*.
"Well?" he looked me up and down. "Symbolical,"
I breathed, not yet knowing the word *cliché*
or bright moments of love's throwaways.

All summer Johnny was prince of the penny arcade,
arms around me on the tilt-a-whirl,
mug-shot grins in the quarter photo booth,
twanging his guitar for street kids on the hill
who scored baggies of hashish and Panama Red

until security cameras zeroed in.
Johnny's stoned effusions never let on
the double-mortgaged double-wide in Renton,
his father on the graveyard shift at Boeing,
his mother scolding my mother on the phone--

his needle tracks my fault, his Dexedrine
knocked back with coke, his hook-ups with *"hookers, maybe
faggots."* The day he brought blonde Suzee
to the Food Court, I sobbed by the Orange Julius machine.
"Stop it," he snapped. "Your mascara's smeared."

I rode north alone to the next rehearsal: *The Tempest*.
Iris, messenger of the gods, weaving the river
spell through tears because the show goes on.
"Clear, concise, poetic," wrote the reviewer
of my part, before he panned the rest.

I went home, tore up Johnny's song, wrote one
and tore it up. If I couldn't be with him
I wouldn't *be* him. I opened the Cambridge edition
of Shakespeare, and told my mother the truth.
I'm starting a poem.

WOMAN BLOOMING FOR THE WIND MACHINE

You were the darling of the movie set
but it couldn't last.
They called you Swan Girl,

Overnight Surprise, the answer
to everybody's wasted life.
Would you do it all again?

Nothing too difficult
in those days, you cantered ponies
through Hyde Park, chartered

a Greek yacht all summer
down the Carolina coast.
Lovers slipped invitations into

the pockets of your Arctic fox.
But you let the doubletalkers
have their way with you. What

started out as sonnet
at the masked ball in Verona
turned to hit list—a wire mobile

built to destroy itself
at the script's first call
for wind. Rumors of gray-suited men

who could pin nothing on you.
Your blonde hair grew out
brown, a stranger's child

was pulled dead out of you,
yours was the body that refused
to sleep. The sun too loud,

the colors of your dresses
turned against you. The gold key
committee in your home town

kept changing the rules.
Everybody but dead lovers
missed the point. What else

was left? You were the debutante
of lost wishes, nothing
in the archives of your new faith

could have saved you.
We looked away
when your closed carriage passed,

older than we'd ever been,
knowing a different river
touched you as you slept.

CULT HERO

"Are you my Angel?"
—*Allen Ginsberg*

After a breakfast of oysters
and champagne, he's out the door,
ready for anything. Sorority curtains
slit open—veils in harems.
Just the sight of him
rubs the fantasy in.

He grins back, kicks a crater
in the Japanese gardener's
tidy Fuji of clippings,
and moves on, practicing
his Merlin walk, thoughts
a few feet off the ground
and nowhere near heaven.

The source of his rhymes—
a voice in San Diego, coming on
after the stations sign off.
His students rehearse his gestures
in their dormitory rooms for hours,
write theses on the five-footed children
he's peopled the town with,

How we'd all love to be
as effortless and public,
our shadows grown sizes larger,
others waiting hours in line
to sign up for our thoughts—
those who put bookmarks in their lives

to follow him. End of the semester
and look where he's brought us—
cloven hooves prancing through the parks,
sun coming out when he claps
obliging us to applaud him.
We never seem to finish
what we came to ask

before he vanishes—Midas
of dactyls—into the aesthetic
distance, everything he's touched
turned aureate, the glitter
in some lost disciple's eye.
The truth, after all,
our best rhetoric.

RETURN TO SENDER?

Elvis, at least, could carry a tune,
or steal it from some blues singer
rediscovered mowing lawns in Georgia.
What about you? Your letters
with stamps glued upside down

pile up, and I keep running
my fingers over the letter opener's
ivory blade. The years
glide by like a sustained vibrato
and what have we learned?

I've always been too much for you
and now others begin to say
Well deserved. That's not important
now. I have my own life,
a different address each year

and a new lover who owes nothing
to anyone. Better than I can say
for you. You always turned over
when we failed at love,
and I sat up all night

applying bruises like dark-blue
body paint to my face.
What good did it do?
You were the child in the tube
tied off, the station

I never tuned in. No future
in dreams loaded with payola.
Too many songs you refused
to play. Too many times
you drove me home, singing

"Who cares?" and *"That's the breaks,"*
tapping your cigarettes on the dash.
Was I waiting for some old hit
single to drop into the glass cage
of the Wurlitzer? *Be strong,*

you told me, shaking your car keys
under the porch light, as if I were
an attack of panic to be gotten over,
and one well-timed comeback
could have made you a star.

AFTER ALL IS SAID AND DONE

I ride past your house, my body
heavy with total recall.
You're on the front steps
with your wife and baby daughter.
I hear you've given her
my name, and your wife's hair
falls to her waist like mine.
Once again you point
to bottles of white pills
beside the bed: Dreams in reverse

years after bar exams and bad trips,
the season you lay flat on a veranda
in Benin, fanned by the malarial
winds of the Gold Coast.
Years after bare-bulb apartments
with my photograph glued
to the mirror, shoeboxes of letters
that told you nothing.
A lifetime since my kitchen swayed
as you broke the news: live

or die. Years after you chose
the hard way, and rode the last bus
out of town, with Kathlamet
fishermen asleep between rivers
and their firewater spawn,
aisle lights making bus windows
a regulation gray, in a country
ashamed of its origins.
We were too alone for the long haul,
we hadn't yet learned

doubt's forwarding addresses.
I, who staked everything
on those first sights of you—
pacing between the metal detection
gates for my return, from London
or Santiago or New York, a cigarette
unlit between your fingers
to break yourself of the habit.
And you, who hitchhiked three hundred miles
in the winter rains to rid yourself

of my name, then turned around
when a trucker outside Nehalem
pulled his .45 and my voice
bloomed from the barrel.
What could we say to each other
now that the tables have been turned?
Years too late to wake up
from whatever I told you I wanted.
You've sat in the medicine circles
between shamans who carved

the spirit poles: ravens and seals
under the rain spell, cured
of the vision called *forever*.
I live with shopping malls
and chemical solutions, my face
trapped in the xerox machine mirror,
victim of its own choices.
How could we speak familiar lines
or return to afternoons
in the false summer ahead of us?

How could we endure the cold salt
of the dunes, that first morning
you parted my legs, as if to silence
the circling drone of the spy plane?
You came home years later
to the law books, and I stared out
the windows. How much did you want
to keep me? Your hand on my thigh
the morning after another man had me.
"Where, to me, has ceased to mean

with whom," you wrote, your last letter
under the broken hands of the compass,
the postmark from Cape Fear.
Even then you dreamed
according to the rules,
and I, who knew nothing
of the heart's diminishing returns,
wandered through the black
and white decor, erasing
your mouth-prints from my body.

AT THE OLYMPIC MUSIC FESTIVAL
AFTER SEEING *AMADEUS*

"Though I than He—may longer live
He longer must—than I"

This isn't quite the Shed at Tanglewood
or Josef of Hapsburg's formal Viennese gardens.
The musicians aren't silk-frocked or jacketed

in their Festival logo T-shirts and baggy Calvins.
They rue the rudeness of suburbanites in barns,
Seattle Symphony docents who snap their flashguns,

their stage whispers upstaging the violins.
Here, no young genius coughs among the marble fauns,
but black-face lambs in the Children's Petting Pens

bleat between (and a perfect fifth below)
Largo cantabile and *Allegro vivo.*
We listeners look around us in the second half—

the ladder to the loft a measure of the great staff,
fusebox tie-wires behind the stalls, the Steinway
rolled to a whole rest against the hay,

where he'd have drunk up the day, copied verbatim
the brain's completed scores. The day's last piece
with its second violin like a secret rival's voice,

is his String Quartet in C, K. 515.
My birthday in two days, I check his dates
as afternoon wind sweeps down off Mount Olympus

like a lifelong *sostenuto:* 1756
to 1791. By the time he was
my age, he'd put the pen down on the *Requiem.*

His notes so flawless we can't explain away
the price, we drive home from this Sunday
music-lovers' farm, with half

our average span of years before us.
The magic piccolo's giggle up the scale:
celestial flourish of his mortal voice

scrawled to a stop in the *lacrimosa's* wail.
What chance for revision in the common grave
in earshot of that reckless laugh?

MILL CREEK RISING

You drive up the valley and walk along
Mill Creek, a concrete-lined channel
of fish ladders, whitewater riffles
regular as breath, the creek much wider here
than downstream, a rivulet steaming
from overheated springs, beside
saddened clapboard houses. Your wife

walked out of your house
years ago, you called her *blank-faced
as the moon.* No warning signals
in that brick and shingle bungalow,
or else you were too busy with science's
hyper-educated guesses, crossing out all
your own equations. *Could I have made*

a truce with my equations, you ask,
years after love's educated gamble
gave way, and you drove to Mill Creek
every evening to live past your mistakes.
Every Christmas, you planted a live tree
for your children, your yard a woodlot
bristling with admonitions from the Brothers

Grimm. Balsam firs shot up in inverse
ratio to your son and daughter's
moving out, your reasons to stay
broke down at the fence line where
the heart's strewn fields began,
the hemlock shadows lengthened.
For years you let the border collie

roam the wheat hills above the dam
while you paced the catwalk over

the spillway, jumped from the irrigation
flume's abutment to the dam's lip.
Long before, at high water, you leapt
from piling to piling across the reservoir
with your infant son in your arms,

giving him what you never knew
you'd missed. Now the catch basin
behind the barrier wall is so full
that water races through sluice gates
under a cirrus-streaked moon like
film run backwards in black and white.
One afternoon you sat in a darkened room

with white pills in your mouth,
waiting for the pharynx muscles
to decide for themselves. Then
you opened the windows and let the all-
day rain go on. *Anything could have
happened after that:* you spent
years in fields where second-growth

prairie grass failed, keeping promises
to your children in their distant cities.
You wanted to ask her, *Did we ever share
the same sky?*, but you climbed alone
into the abandoned treehouse
in the willows. Moonlight spilled
cool over your shoulders, the river

moved like memory's true fires between
your life and what you wanted
to happen, breaking into fractions on
the man-made lake, runoff wrack trapped
in the dam's weir where last summer's
lovers took off their clothes
under a heaven restless with signs.

NIGHT WALK AROUND GREEN LAKES

Above Hancock Field, light keeps on
arriving in stars' past formations.
Late jets circle in the holding patterns,

Syracuse glows over the horizon
like a dying sun. The engines' roar
lags behind, cone of a noise

pointed backwards: silence,
landing lights advancing on the night.
Silence, too, where the Pleiades,

misty sisters, huddle under
the sky's dome, where the ancients
watched huge gladiators wheel

and stride down the dark ecliptic.
At midnight, the jewels in Orion's belt
glitter through the smog.

Let's ask the few owls left
for wisdom, save some inflections
from the clipped shriek of a mouse.

When we go, we take our tail lights
with us, fuel exhaust streaming
behind us like Andromeda's veil.

As if Diogenes, old Cynic,
had thrust his lamp into our faces,
left us dazed; then stumped away,

hefting his receding light,
we slam the car doors, shift
into position, turn out of the driveway.

All night, the Great Bears
circle each other in the sky.

A SLOW NIGHT IN THE SUBURBS

Rustle of acacia by the gate,
traffic roar fading down Baseline.
All the soft turning lights
on the hair styles of dancers,
mirrors behind the bar repeating
everything that glitters
and is far away. Here,
darkness and the whirr
of the ceiling fan, before
the telephone rings at midnight
with the truth. Weren't they lovely
the last few hours you believed
his excuses and kept your world?
From now on, stains in the wallpaper
will blame you, the lock on the safe
deposit box the burglars missed.
The view out the kitchen window
just another trap for the senses.
All the American sunsets,
wide-open spaces you swore
you'd never run out of, more reasons
to avoid the issue: Running's a habit
some people never break.
Already you see your shadow
miles ahead of him, losing itself
over the state line, the western
edge of the time zone.

EXURBAN SPELL

"Thousands of acres of American farmland are lost each year
to suburban and exurban housing development."
—*National Public Radio*

The children dream of pre-fab houses
going up in the cornfields, wallboard
in rising tiers, hingeless doorjambs
propped against the siding,
no handles anywhere. Families
stream out from the megalopolis
to buy, and move in before the paint dries.

All night the children wander
across the wall-to-wall lawns
of living rooms, wondering
how to stop the ghosts
of bulltoads, crop roots writhing
underneath their beds.

In the dens of tract homes, wives
fold up the children's things, husbands
close their *Newsweeks* for the evening.
Constellations glitter overhead
like Hallowe'en hags' eyes, the moon
swollen as a 4-H gourd. Tendrils

of green beans curl over fences,
fingers of familiar spirits.
Their pods bang heavily as fists
against the screen doors.
The one pumpkin passed over by the backhoe
blows up quietly, fills a whole yard.

Kernels creep into the rank
and file of furrows, and go to work
on their dragons'-teeth maneuvers.
The grown corn waves its silo-high tassels
at the moon.
                              Exurban wives yawn.
Husbands turn off their VCR's
and stumble obediently to bed. All

night they dream uneasily
while the runners of sweet peas
tighten their noose-holds on the doorknobs,
and cattails ringing the garden
sharpen their green swords on the moon.

THE CUSTODY OF THE EYES

"The Eye sees more than the Heart knows"

—William Blake

THE LOVELIEST COUNTRY OF OUR LIVES

Trains crawled from the stations
slow as the locomotives
in last century's tintypes.
North Dakota stretched away, a long
genealogy of wheat. We travelers slept
as the cars gathered speed, hurtled forward
between fields and the memory
of fields . . .
                        At Glendive we awakened
and stared into moon-dry arroyos
as if for the question our dreams
kept trying all afternoon to ask,
like passengers who gesture through
plate glass to children smiling
and shrugging from the platform.

The question had something to do
with buttes rising and falling
like waves of an inland sea,
the warm Paleocene of our recollection:

What was it we were going to become?

Cottonwood leaves went on quaking,
nodding agreement with every assertion
of the wind. The question blended imperceptibly
with its answer like a life continuing,
an ocean of fields slowly drained
of wheat.
                        We shifted position, the moon
fixed in mid-heaven, instructing travellers
in the reliability of light.

The train crossed the Missouri
on its steel trestle. The water
was rippling and wheat-colored,
a dream of river with an answer
for every memory of fields.

We were passing through
the loveliest country of our lives.

FARM OUTSIDE OSWEGO

"The pure products of America..."
—*William Carlos Williams*

Amidst the jumble of half-lived lives—
gutted chairs, rusted Westinghouses
piled in sheds, cattle shelters crumbling
under half a century of wind—
the fat farm wife played Scrabble,
selecting each piece carefully
as if she held it up to an egg light.
Her grown son, out from town,
lounged with his coffee, craned
to watch words branch out on the board.

Begging their pardons, we'd stepped in
from the *Retired Racehorses for Sale*
sign faded by the stable, asked
to use the john, Sunday drivers
who'd stopped on a whim that lingered
from our long, horse-crazy girlhoods.
We wiped our hands on streaked towels.
The Franklin stove glowered as we passed.

The farm wife picked another letter
with a connoisseur's deliberation.
Outside, flatbeds driven into pasture
for the last time drowned in the timothy,
and rusted tractor hulls
surrounded the new, alfalfa-green John Deere
like chokecherry on apple trunks.
Holstein heifers stared
from hock-deep mire by the barn.
The farm cur groveled, the whipped look
white in the corners of his eyes.

We visited the founder-crippled pony,
the stable's sole remaining tenant,
last. We gazed at his curled,
Aladdin-slipper hooves, the stagger
as he wove, barn-bound,
from side to side of his stall.
As we left, we did not pat him:
What would have changed it?

In the house, Scrabble fragments
jostled for attention,
strangle-vines for the sun.
The woman remembered, moved
for the stove, the clumsy loaves
hot on her reddened hands.
At the back door, oat mash for the Angusses,
supper sandwiches arranged like letters
on the smorgasbörd. After the animals,
they would eat in silence, farm-style.

We started down the dirt track to the car,
the ancient thoroughbred racers
long since auctioned from the stalls.
The son slipped out the back door
with the pail, past pine poles
stacked fresh as a vocabulary
of good intentions. He gazed after us,
face blank as the space between
two words. We waved. He raised one hand,
gabbled once, as if wooden letters
were log-jammed in his throat.
Then turned and trudged toward fences
downed years ago by the wind.

AFTER WE RECEIVED THE NEWS
OF THE 100-MILE WIND

Laramie to Cheyenne

We thought the first lines we sent out
would cover it—our stolen children
gathered into the apron of the wind—
but this gale chilled the farthest corners
of our meaning. Empty hopper cars

lifted lightly as balsa off the tracks
and our first warning—a warmth
with a threatening undercurrent to it—
was confirmed. All over town, children
were opening drawers, pulling jackets
from closets, hurrying down walks
as if to the bus stop. Fists burrowing

their pockets for the proper change,
they didn't notice how their parents' feet
were rooted to the porches, their hands
gnarling in the very act of waving *Wait!*
Come back! Across the prairies,

wind revved up its engines,
sucked in darkness like a fuel.
The children vanished
over the horizon. We drew our hands back,
the last in a genealogy of shadows.
Nothing we could have offered
would ever have been enough.

CROSSING THE DIVIDE

I Montana

The hills around Three Forks explode with yellow,
heather or toadflax
or some roadside weed whose name
I don't remember. I relish such easy
familiarity with names,
even as I let go, finally,
of the right to call yours—
to find the perfect nomenclature
for your body, to say, "This
I understand, belong to by the rights of loving."

Doubt passed by on its whirlwind tour.
We welcomed it, thought it was the developer
we'd hardly expected quite so soon.
It took the titles from us;
they fell from our hands
the way dry leaves crumble
in a relentless heat.

The pages of the calendar won't turn over
since the day we drove off
in different moving vans, our
lives going on forever
over opposite horizons.

II *A Second Growth*

The bus begins the long climb to the Divide.
The continent shelves away,
each valley extending into an aspen and pasture distance
like someone else's Promised Land.

A U-Haul labors past.
Its driver has fierce moustaches,
scowls with concentration.
Children romp on the cab seat.
The heavy woman raises an arm
to strike one whose mouth gapes
in a silent shriek or laugh
and then they are past me.

                      I'd swear the mountains have grown
more immense, the pines more squat,
hunkering into the leesides of a bitter wind.
Rock breaks in striations,
the streams begin their falls toward opposing oceans.
Not even subalpine firs can hide it,
standing upright on the crags
with all the courage of a second growth.

Someone, a traveler or migrant worker
maybe, has scrawled "Yucatán" upon a rock—
a claim, an attempt to recollect a family,
a neolithic cry: *Socorro.*

A letter going nowhere home.

ANOTHER LOOK AT "ALBION ON THE ROCK": PLATE 38 OF BLAKE'S *MILTON*

"Turn away no more;
"Why wilt thou turn away?
"The starry floor,
"The wat'ry shore,
"Is giv'n thee till the break of day."
—William Blake, *Songs of Experience*

The naked lovers sprawl on a *"wat'ry shore."*
His right hand fingers, absently, the sea
slapping at its tidal mark. His left hand
keeps moving over her thigh. Why? His love
has swelled and ebbed, he turns his head away.
So close they could almost touch it above their bed

An eagle swoops . . . Once I lay in your king-sized bed,
embracing you like that woman on the shore.
I'd thrown caution, like a no-deposit can, away,
and chattered on about the all-surrounding sea
as the poets' emblem of unfettered love.
You turned over, yawning into your hand.

"What do you see in the lifelines on your hand?"
I asked. "Nothing about you," you said. Our bed,
it seems, a momentary lapse—an excuse for love
we'd dropped between us like a net, to shore
up our sands from dissolving in an alien sea
before some reclamation bureau dredged the tide away.

Since then I've moved time and tidal zones away
and you're the developer on TV whose hand
sweeps back to reveal the view lots by the sea,

the blueprints scattered on some happy couple's bed.
You know the cost of each square inch of shore,
call a good investment "Your finest act of love."

What was I but an early draft of love?
Your contractors changed the woman, hauled away
birdlife, trees—all but the cost-effective shore.
I've owned up to the deeds passing through my hands,
detain no wheeler-dealers in my bed
and sign all petitions to preserve the sea.

No engraving saves or replicates the sea—
the etching crude, ink gouaches *gauche* as love
between *True Confession's* covers. One printer's bed
laid wrong upsets the whole edition. Ages away,
Blake, hell-bent, shook his stylus hand
at heaven. I X-out houses on protected shores.

The poet cried, "Turn away no more!" The sea
falls and rises again in its bed between shores,
and love is our wealth. It holds nothing in its hands.

DARWIN'S HOUSE AT DOWNE (CLOSED FRIDAYS)

"A serious house on serious earth it is. . ."
—Philip Larkin

". . . whilst this planet has gone cycling on according
to the fixed law of gravity, from so simple a beginning
endless forms most beautiful and most wonderful
have been, and are being, evolved."
—Charles Darwin, *On the Origin of Species*

We knew for whom was built this special shell
and for whom kept. We knew the dates,
the names; we'd pictured ourselves

for years, sitting at the master's desk,
walking his routes between fields
beyond the wrought-iron gates.

Even stones along the paths—
knapped flint chipped from walls
by the hedge trimmers—had mental

analogues. We'd reasoned so long
from other thinkers' universals
that only the unlisted quirky schedules

of English country houses
could cancel out our plans
like a cold tide over Permian bogs.

Anomalous as the hours on the plaque
were our thoughts—the work
of some thick-brained sublunar hack

setting off half-cocked to prove
the obvious: we'd trusted to luck
and the survival of the forty-hour week.

We'd failed our direction-seeking species.
All day we wandered the village's
hedge-blind lanes, where magpies

fussed in the dying hawthornes' crowns
and ponies put their ears back in alarm
at unseen guard dogs patrolling the farm

and only we had no natural enemies.
What question had we not adapted
to our failure? We turned at the rusted

warning signs, no wiser than if the door
had opened on glass cases of fossils,
faded letters, specimens; a study

restored to its original, untitled
clutter; and some neighboring lord's
cache of stuffed, exotic birds,

iridescence on their wings pristine
where autumn's unfaked sunlight falls.
Squinting at the facts' dusty particulars

as scholars do, we would have missed
the truth of all small complicated
objects under glass, our interest

trapped in its own success
like a band of shaggy Pleistocene ponies
whose clifftop pasture shrinks

into the surrounding arms of ice.
This was our life, the bones say.
No matter the brain's methodic fever.

The laboratory in ruins,
the big elms gone, we drove off
past the NO ADMITTANCE doors

back to our childless, *fin de siècle*
rooms, wondering what would become
of our kind—taking the fixed laws

so lightly, rushing in ever-smaller cars
down the widening flow of motorway,
as we matched names on the maps

to houses older than our country,
as if scraps of someone else's history
could make us whole: a species

teetering at the top of its form,
where evolution stopped a moment.
Then moved on.

ESCAPE FROM THE MUSEUM

The guard in the room full of stone fruit
loomed over your shoulder,
tapping his nightstick, telling you
Get back. Dogs in Etruscan murals
snarled, their eyes whitened
with the urge to lunge.
You could have lost yourself
in some Gothic scene, the Virgin's mantle,
Quattrocento sky.

Wall spaces were marked
"Removed for Restoration."
In the Egyptian room,
dead tongues turned to gold,
a 4,000-year-old Pharaoh
bound hand and foot upon his throne.
Under the knowing looks
of gargoyles, you walked out
with your unforgiven past.

Waiting at the Green Line's
first above-ground stop,
you tried to wish the train
out of the tunnel, under
the intersection's crossed wires,
the intricacies of speech.
The lover impossible
to argue with or please.

Love was carried on here
with a deadly propriety—
your fiancé of a few days
instructing you how to breathe

in public. The free American
air. On the outbound train,
you could feel the strangle
of mink at your throat.

You climbed to the narrow shadows
of your room, threw yourself down
in a mauve indifference,
and drifted, giving Saturday
time to gather itself
for the Sabbath, for the mink
to claw its way from the furrier's
kennel, the bloodied civil trap.

INDIAN COUPLE HAVING AN ARGUMENT

On the subway platform, jammed
with Saturday pleasure-seekers,
she picked at the pleats
of her sari, exhaustion

leaving its caste-mark.
He turned away, crushing
packages for the child
growing heavier inside her.

Nard and orange groves stretched away
across the low hills behind her eyes.
Her younger sisters leaned over
the veranda, waving goodbye,
silks billowing in coastal wind.

He sighed, thought of the whir
of air conditioners, blueprints
unrolled in the high-rises.
He looked back: her father's cheque
from Bombay, the ochre-daubed Brahmin
who joined their hands soon after,
the magenta veil not yet lifted
from her face.

                She remembered
the taxi at dawn through the strange,
metallic city, the apartment's
bare walls—the first silence
that held no family in it.

They faced each other: the blueprints,
drone of the *Dharma Sutra,* eyes opening
in the paisley of her pleats.
                            The child
kicked for the first time inside her.

A CONJECTURAL GUIDE TO
DUNSTANBURGH CASTLE

Northumberland Coast

We climbed over the stile into a field
where shaggy cattle watched us through the mist.
Around us, green slopes; below, the fog-bound sea.
Beyond, grey skeleton fingers of stone
rose, like a Saxon king's farewell, from the ruin
crowning the hill of Dunstanburgh Castle.

This coast is bound by a chain of failed castles
that couldn't keep the dragon-prowed sea-
chariots away: tide-breachers, ruin-
work of warriors in cowhorn helmets, fields
stripped, villages burned down to the stone
before the Norsemen's ships vanished through the mist.

We almost glimpsed their ghost-sails through mist
where thick surf heaved against shingle stones
below the cliff's sheer plummet. Surely a castle
bastioned on this crag would be spared from ruin!
But it prevailed against phalanxes of empty fields
and fog closing in from the muffled sea.

What undermined it finally was the sea,
kingdom of salt, corrosive tide that ruins
all it conquers. The villagers moved their fields
inland, and stole back under night's cloak of mist
to help themselves to what was left of the castle.
The parish filled with barns of fine-cut stone,

and houses, kirks. Why waste, they thought, good stone?
So curtain walls melted to the level of the field
and the broken barbican's fingers clawed the mist.
How could they know there'd be an interest in old castles,
that strangers would trudge this cow track by the sea
and pay good sterling to clamber on a ruin?

The ticket booth was closed all winter at the ruin,
but someone forced the gate. What we knew of castles
our sole guide to these unmarked stones,
we feigned rebuilding the slumped towers and sea-
tumbled steps that ended in blank walls of mist
as sun withdrew like a weak ally from the field.

Mist unfurled its banners from the ruin,
the North Sea hushed on the heraldic stones.
Viking shadows gathered in fields before the castle.

LOGOS OF THE SENTIMENTALIST

Did you believe it when I said
the sixth sense was up
to its old tricks again?

I lied: a little story, harmless
as greeking on illustrators' signboards,
gossip passed from ear to ear
at party games, unrecognizable
as our own voices at the end.

Like children, we said we didn't ask
to be born. Someone else was in charge
of real mistakes, someone else
would do all the forgetting.

Now, I linger in dress shops
past closing, unable to buy
or go away unchanged.
I get fortune cookies on the first date—
She Who Hesitates is Lost.

Area codes gather in the air
to judge me by their distance.
Men for whom I box up
and mail my life, telling myself
nothing lasts forever.

You always counted your outbound fare,
opened windows to enlarge the room,
reminding me you could still get away
in time. I shook the alarm clock
to rattle lost hours out
like Lake Tahoe dollars.

Variations in our stories
shifted like stars in a planetarium sky,
dragons and scorpions swirling into focus
in the galactic haze.

No dust so radiant when houselights
came up over the grubby loges,
and aging young mothers sat
beside children begging for black-hole
blasters and laser-beam TV's,
the zodiac gone one sign beyond
their chances. In your version

there was a boy alone
in the back row with unexplained
blood on his hands. In mine,
the little girl who knew
exactly what she was doing.

Meanwhile, no one kept track
of the contradictions, or had courage
to connect the dots and ask *What's
wrong with this picture?*

I confess, I've never filled in
the missing years, or figured out
whose name it was you called me by.
I only pretended to see my own face
out of focus, or hear your telephone
ring in other women's houses.

I hang on to my excuses
while your letters fill with questions
and spiderweb light widens
on the windows. It's my fault
if I can't accept the moon
that goes on foraging the sky.

WALK IN MID-WINTER: REVISITING THE SCENE

This landscape always in eclipse—
dirt lanes that lose themselves
in the scrub of subdivisions.
Cumulus mauve with the lights
of a distant city. Declining stars.

When the last bus swerves at the turn,
we stop in spatter of the embankment.
Suburbs wait for late commuters
at the end of the line
and night, like a dangerous neighbor
moves in next hill over.

The cold stars fling remnants
of their light down the sky
and we return to the truth that gives us
back to ourselves, outsiders now,
a radiance stealing across our faces—
memory's equinoctial precession.

It's not the roar of headlights
gunning down walkers at the curves,
not night-blind watchdogs howling
into silence at the end of their chains,
not children peering from the warm tableaux
of kitchens that muster the battalions
of porch lights against us,

but that in the hemlock darkness
of a clearing at the edge of town
we are no strangers to the absences
that line up quietly inside us.

No one knows we move in shadow,
under constellations so brilliant
they could have seared us home.

LAST DREAM IN PERÚ

Lake Titicaca

It was my job
to mimic the crane's cry
as my friends and I skiffed
through the estuary reeds.
But how could I, unless my life
beat in the heart of the bird
and looked through his eye?
My own name was all
I could call.

As they rowed, my friends told me
how, under the floors of their cabins,
they'd excavated old stone walls
whose joints were still
as mortarless and smooth as faces
without memories or dreams.

All I meant to say went quiet.
Real cranes cried
above the thin wind.

It was time to turn back
to land. Before we reached
the shore, I'd have to find
an opening in the water
that fit my speech,
and whisper my name in it
before the lake closed over
and sank it like a stone.

WALK TO THE RUSSIAN
MONASTERY GARDEN

"I sleep, but my heart waketh."
—from the *Philokalia*

Uneasy dreams pried me open.
A shrine, a vigil light, veiled women
turned back at the gate.
The season held me accountable

for everything I knew.
I left your sleep, walked
away from darkened windows
to the monastery road, my guardians

the winter constellations.
December flowers knifed the air,
the long night frozen on its stem.
I took my own breath in my hands

The stars threw down their weapons.
I stepped through the orchard's
dark, Cyrillic branches, wondered
at the crossing of our lives.

In your wintry city, I was lost
in the wordless drifts. I stood
among shadows of apple trunks,
silence's long hands across the snow.

SAINT PETERSBURG UPON THE NEVA

These White Nights glow, midsummer's dusky sheen upon the river.
Gold Domes of the Resurrection mirror Spilled Blood's
           gleam upon the river.

The Bronze Steed rears on his granite cliff above
           the mythic serpent's coils.
Great Peter spurs him: hoofprints sink into winter's
           iron screen upon the river.

Where goes Raskolnikov? Outside his dusty flat, graffiti
           in the stairwell asks
"Where's the axe?" How many steps to where it drains
           its spleen upon the river?

Pushkin's young wife at her needlepoint as the dueling
           pistols stutter.
His death mask and her dancing slippers in shadow-minuet
           careen upon the river.

On the Mariinsky's stage, Boris Godunov glides in filigree,
           his coronation cage,
Mourning for ancient Rus, the traitor's scheme upon the river.

In the Summer Garden, the boy Nabokov drops his mesh net
           over monarchs' wings.
Marble fauns tilt their pinions toward him—pre-Revolutionary
           dream upon the river.

Akhmatova in a black shawl intones her *Requiem*—Russia's
           grieving queen at her window in Fontanny Dom.
Her guest from England marvels, but Stalin pounds his fist—
           writers' graves grow green upon the river.

Leningrad's 900 days burn in the eternal flame at Piskaryov.
The nameless dead nestle under grass, their memories
　　　　an ashen scene upon the river.

Hey, word mangler! Waken from your gilded, inlaid daze,
　　　　　　stroll with poets
From the Idiot to The Stray Dog, footsteps measured
　　　　　　by vodka's golden mean upon the river.

AS I DRIVE OVER AN IRRIGATION DITCH
AT THE END OF SUMMER, I THINK OF
A SMALL-TOWN AMERICAN PREACHER

(with apologies to James Wright)

> Where is the sea, that once
> solved the whole loneliness
> of the Midwest?
> —*Written A.D.* 1960

Preacher Bob, half-cracked old trouble-maker,
what's the point?
I think of you,
unsteady, hoisting the Good Book aloft
on the brown lawns of Mid-America State U.
while you're being dragged by your hanks
heavenward like a sinner
in the hands of a pissed-off god.
You'll make it, I guess,
by millennium's end.

But it is 1999, it is almost the season
for Y2K, and the backyard oil pumps of Central Oklahoma
keep salaaming like iron locusts toward the East,
appeasing the prophets of OPEC.
Where is that born-again coed
whom you called a jezebel?
Where are your catalogues in which you lay
Victoria's Secrets bare? your rantings
of everlasting fire on women's flowered panties?
We know what happened to the sea,
and with the ozone layer doing its strip-tease
heating up this Eden of greenhouse gasses,
the sea has promised: *I will come again.*

Where will the Midwest be then, Bob,
and will you still be lonely? I can see nothing
of the hot air that bloweth
where it listeth of your preaching.
The synod that subsidizes you to heckle the hell-bound
stays tastefully out of view
and no one in the multitude jeering at your jeremiads
is your friend.
                              When the trumpet blares
for the millennial shutdown
will any of the Holy City's twelve gates
open to your access code?
Or will you be standing there
between the charred hulls of the grain elevator
and the football stadium, like a nuclear shadow
burned into a wall at ground zero,
holding the end of a shorted power cord
for a thousand years?

Born under the sign of Cancer,
I knew I'd die of it.
Horoscopes were against me,
and sky maps in the newspaper
featured the Crab stars every Sunday.

That was the hushed-up Fifties,
after Bikini Atoll and the Big C,
and they'd just found strontium-
90 in the milk. It smelled
like weapons. I tried to figure out

the tropics, running their 23 1/2
degree circles around the globe.
The one up north
would get me. I envied my father
his Capricorn birthday.

Later, I read Henry Miller
for a clue, until my father came in
one night, pulled back the bedsheets
and snapped the flashlight off.
I still seek that known latitude.

I boycott Replogle products,
wear Linus Pauling T-shirts,
and teach my parrot to say
Ban the Bomb.
I telephone Madame Noor,

my chartmaker, for a reading.
She tunes in the celestial sphere,
my stars line up.
She shakes her head, warns me
not to read the *National Enquirer*

for a cure. She says, "Think of the disease
you're most afraid of, dream yourself
dying, healed of it forever."
I imagine myself empty
between collarbone and hip,

sunlight falling in long arcs
where an arm was. I say things
about the nuclear family,
buy mushrooms and make detonation noises
as I slice them, never use

words like *metastasize* and *remission,*
even when I'm going through a change
of subject, or trying to move out
on sin. To date, I have no symptoms.
I have nothing in common with children

lying in their tents of pure breath
at the Mayo Clinic,
their charts fixed at the angles
of declining stars, Three Mile Island
glowing through their sleep.

CLOSING THE CIRCLE

Blown every which way
by those who believe in wind,
you settle for the dreams
at hand: the horseshoe crab's
trajectory, ripple patterns
having second thoughts, foghorns
summoning each other all night.
Lovers who've missed their connections.

You get up later every morning,
the clock that burglarized your sleep
rusting among salt-spray roses
by the window. You forget yourself,
put on coffee for the lover
who walked out, his portrait
erasing itself from the canvas.

All day, drawers open and close
in your thoughts. Your palette knives
dictate policy, you bring to found objects
an incredible belief.
The peacock eyes in the murals
are on to every move you make.

At sunset, you deck yourself out
for men who promise to supply
the other half of what you're thinking.
You mix a little anguish
in the vodka. This time,
you tell yourself, no one's
going to change the locks.

There have got to be alternatives
for going backwards into love.
You peer through rose-colored
apertures, recite unlisted numbers
by which you could repaint
your future. Outside,

wind mounts its assault and battery
on the harbor. You throw an old quilt
on the battleship-gray floor
and call your fears home.
All night, the pure pigments
close their circle
at the easel's unfinished borders.

"IF THIS IS WEDNESDAY, IT MUST BE VIENNA"

After a leisurely breakfast, we left the hotel
with our guidebook to explore the city.
The maps were well-drawn, and explained in our language
where the castle and old walls used to be, before the changes
wrought by several wars, new currency
and laws, and the recent popularity of travel.

In winter, it's not so popular to travel,
so there we were, asking directions in their language
and being answered in our own, counting a different currency
each week, returning, when museums closed, to the hotel
to rest, read the *Herald-Tribune* for changes
in the dollar, decide which restaurant to try in the city.

Sometimes all the cities blurred into one city
and we recalled our schoolbook French: *Plus ça change
plus c'est la même chose.* The aphorist makes fun of his travels,
no one knows the real value of currency,
and we spent half our waking hours in hotels,
washing, dressing, arguing whether languages

affect the brain, or the brain languages.
Our dollars talked, and English was the strongest currency
in every bank or tourist shoppe or new hotel
that crowded more local people out of the city.
We were ashamed of our countrymen who, when they travel,
complain loudly about everything. "Let the world change

for us!" Their voices went up like high-rises. And so it changes,
while we vanished down narrow streets near our hotel,
pretending we were back in the quaint medieval city
which was merely cramped and dirty then, when travel
was what ragged minstrels sang of in strange languages
stained with the blood on Crusaders' currency.

Their god's saving power was spent, before currency
they plundered could convert—by sword or travel
home, where no one cared how much they'd changed—
to stone and stained glass, those costly languages.
Now, we redeem the accounts of those storied cities
with airports and parking lots and big hotels.

Someday these cities may be nothing but hotels
and only currency will translate, by computers, to their language.
Who then, by travel in those days, shall be changed?

A MEMORY OF ISLANDS

The old country woman wailed
and leaned her head against the wall.
Black-scarved godmothers clustered
to restrain her, murmuring
in high voices of village widows.
Swallows settled at dusk
on telegraph wires of their girlhoods.
The black-edged telegrams
had showed them early who they were.

In the ward, her husband drifted
on the white sea of the sheets,
forgetting the sky over Inishmore,
wharves where he mended nets
with his brothers. Shadows at noon
blue through village windows, his wife
turning toward him from the courtyard.

By now the priest had come.
He crossed himself before he entered,
carrying the Gifts. He bent to listen,
heard the ticking of inner clocks,
remembered how they grew gigantic
in silence—the time he gazed
all night at the cross
and knew his own face
would someday fill with shadows.

The woman hung on the drift
of her husband's breath, repeating
his name like a rosary, a plea
before the saint's face for a sign. Outside,
the radiant memory of islands.

He floated beneath the oxygen's
clear dome. The priest's voice
reached him like a dream from shore,
a message through an anechoic chamber.
His hand closed over the cross
the priest held toward him
as if it were a tiller. Around him
silence kept on glowing
as it had to underwater,
holding its breath forever.

CLAIRVOYANT'S READING

Unlock the Sphinx, she tells me, there's
a yellow scent for miles.
Roman sculptures cluster on the hills.
The Archer draws his crossbow
over the observatory dome.
At the field's edge, an Arab pony
paws the mustard flowers. Pyramids
glisten in blood-begotten light.

Mustard flowers at the field's edge,
centaur over the observatory dome.
Sandalpaste and turmeric, she tells me,
from the sacrifice of fire. Pyramids
glisten in blood-begotten light
where the Archer draws his crossbow.
And the woman you once were
poises at the casement, listening

for the Arab pony's neigh, a message
from the sacrifice of fire.
Where are the sculptures that crowned
the Palatine? The Bronze Age guides
who walked among us with their javelins,
their granite, anachronistic lions?
Their yellow scent clings, their blood-
begotten mustard flowers glisten.

Listen: the woman you once were
hands you keys to unfamiliar doors.
The guide to the Bronze Age leads you
to the waterline mirrored in hemlocks'
downward shadows, where the Centaur

and the Arab pony graze. Sandalpaste
and turmeric—runes on the observatory
dome, foretellings from the sacrifice of fire.

Stone lions on the steps, the Alexandrian
Library burns to the waterline, weathervanes
stop spinning. The woman poises at the casement,
hands you her keys and parasol. A mustard sun
sets over the Adriatic. Have you been reading
Plutarch's *Lives?* The Bronze Age hemlocks
wrap you in their shadows. What is behind you
is forgiven. Now go, unlock the Sphinx.

THE CUSTODY OF THE EYES

"Those who love uprightness of life
diligently guard their eyes
from all inordinate glancing about."
—St. Bonaventure, *Speculum Disciplinae ad Novitios*

It's the lie I've grown used to.
My plainclothes sisters still negotiate
the cut-rate aisles of the world
in their impeccable habits.
They march according to the anthems,
spines straight as hardback editions.
Their glances veer neither to the romance
nor the crime, their right brains
know not what their lefts are doing.
They have learned perfectly
the Custody of the Eyes.

I

don't have such advantages,
born so astigmatic the stars
never blinked at the proceedings.
In dreams, I follow the right-turn signs
that go left. The Japanese have a verb
for the way I lean toward one companion
or the other as I walk.

In my aquarium,
young flounders' bottom eyes
migrate. Adult, they look up to heaven
double from the bottom-colored
up-side of their bodies.
I, too, have practiced
the Migration of the Eye.

First grade,
the ophthalmologist brought back
my wandering left eye
like a lost sheep: I put hundreds
of cartoon birds in cages, threaded red beads
through rose-colored windows. Every morning
I crossed my eyes like a devotion.

Every ball on the playground
aimed for my plate-glass lenses.
In the class photograph, I'm the one
with the Captain Kidd patch,
my good girl's curl falling
straight in the middle of my forehead.

Thirty years, my pupils still round
and innocent as integers,
mascara on the lashes
fussy as parents who never approved
of contacts. The fiancé who wouldn't pass
the wire-rims, who told me
Take Them Off.

I did.
He stumbled in the sudden blur.
I imagine he wanders still, calls
what he thinks my name is,
holding his aviator shades before him
like a flashlight in Hades.

Now the left side of my skull aches
when that weak eye loses faith.
I make pilgrimages to strange cities,
Basilicas crammed with bad
Italian statues: St. Lucy
carrying her eyeballs in a trencher.

I look both ways.
When no one's watching, I steal them
like a coffee kitty's loose change.

Back home, I drop the eyeballs
in the flounders' cloudy water,
listen for the telephone
to accuse me, ringing the syllables
of my lost love's name.
I glue a postcard on the notebook
from which I have erased
his number: St. Lucy holding a lamp
before her in the dark.

                    I lay me down,
to dream of the lofty Madonna
of my assumptions. I take off my spectacles,
cross the side-arms, turn out the light.
Sisters, I pray, let your glances
trespass in my direction.

I renounce old Argus and his many eyes.

NOTES ON THE POEMS

"Love Affair in a Small Town" is for Lyn.

"Clamming at Tahuya" is for Helena Hileman.

"The Ice-Climber" is for Joseph Maier.

"Historical Site": The General Sherman tree in Sequoia National Park is the largest of the giant sequoia trees (*Sequoiadendron gigantea*), and the most massive living thing on earth. In an earlier era, a tunnel for cars was cut through the trunk of one sequoia so that tourists in motorcars could drive through it and marvel.

"Woman Blooming for the Wind Machine" is in memory of Jean Seberg.

"After All is Said and Done" is for David.

"At the Olympic Music Festival After Seeing *Amadeus*" is for my brother.

"After We Received the News of the 100-Mile Wind" is for my mother.

"Escape from the Museum" is for Jeanne.

"Last Dream in Perú" owes thanks to Jon Lang.

In "Saint Petersburg Upon the Neva," the ghazal's final, signature couplet (*makhta*), addresses the poet in an ironic subversion of the surname (meaning "maker") as "mangler." This poem is with thanks to Mikhail Iossel.

"Closing the Circle" is inspired by the sculptures of Harriet Pappas.

"*If This is Wednesday, It Must Be Vienna*" is in memory of Elizabeth Bishop.

"Clairvoyant's Reading" owes thanks to Jane Bradley, and is in memory of Mrs. Tice. It is for Julia Rowe Hooper Ball, my great-grandmother, County Wicklow, Eire.

"The Custody of the Eyes" is for Madeline DeFrees.

ACKNOWLEDGMENTS

Grateful acknowledgment is made to the following periodicals in which many of these poems first appeared:

American Poetry Review: "Farm Outside Oswego"
Arts & Letters: "Mill Creek Rising," "Crossing the Divide"
The Bloomsbury Review: "After We Received the News of the 100-Mile Wind"
Chattahoochee Review: "At the Olympic Music Festival After Seeing *Amadeus,*"
    "Cult Hero," "Walk in Mid-Winter: Revisiting the Scene"
Chelsea: "A Conjectural Guide to Dunstanburgh Castle," "Darwin's House at
    Downe (Closed Fridays)," "The Ice-Climber"
Crazyhorse: "After All is Said and Done"
Cream City Review: "Night Walk Around Green Lakes," "Return to Sender?"
Harvard Review: "Another Look at 'Albion on the Rock': Plate 38 of Blake's
    Milton"
Helicon Nine: "Indian Couple Having an Argument"
Indiana Review: "Closing the Circle"
The Iowa Review: "Clairvoyant's Reading"
Iron Horse Literary Review: "Last Dream in Perú"
The Journal: "The Loveliest Country of Our Lives"
Michigan Quarterly Review: "Exurban Spell"
Missouri Review: "Under the Sign of Cancer"
New England Review: "A Reply to Storms in New Orleans"
Nimrod: "The Custody of the Eyes," "Farm Outside Oswego"
North American Review: "Studies with Miss Bishop," "Clamming at Tahuya"
    as ("Herons at Tahuya")
Open Places: "A Slow Night in the Suburbs" (as "American Still Life")
Paterson Literary Review: "*Bildungsgedicht*"
Ploughshares: "After the Explosion of Mount St. Helens, The Retiring Grade
    School Teacher Goes for a Long Walk Through the Wheatlands"
Prairie Schooner: "A Memory of Islands," "Walk to the Russian Monastery
    Garden"
Puerto del Sol: "Unfinished Country"
Southern California Anthology: "Darwin's House at Downe (Closed Fridays)"
The Southern Review: "Saint Petersburg Upon the Neva" (as "Ghazal: Saint
    Petersburg Upon the Neva")
Virginia Quarterly Review: "Woman Blooming for the Wind Machine,"
    "Historical Site"
West Branch: "Escape from the Museum"
Western Humanities Review: "'If This is Wednesday, It Must Be Vienna'"
Women's Review of Books: "As I Drive Over an Irrigation Ditch at the End of
    Summer, I Think of a Small-Town American Preacher"

"Celebration for the Cold Snap," "A Change of Maps," "Logos of the Sentimentalist," "LoveAffair in a Small Town," and "Return to Seattle: Bastille Day" first appeared in *Poetry*. Copyright © 1981, 1985, 1986, 1990 by the Modern Poetry Association.

"Celebration for the Cold Snap," "Under the Sign of Cancer," and "The Custody of the Eyes" were reprinted in the anthology *New American Poets of the 80's*, edited by Jack Myers and Roger Weingarten. Wampeter Press, 1984.

"Return to Seattle: Bastille Day" was reprinted in the anthology *Walk on the Wild Side: Contemporary Urban American Poetry*, edited by Nicholas Christopher. Scribner's Sons/Collier Books, 1994.

"Clairvoyant's Reading" was reprinted in the anthology *The Book of Irish-American Poetry from the 18th Century to the Present*, edited by Daniel Tobin. University of Notre Dame Press, 2005.

"A Slow Night in the Suburbs" (as "American Still Life") and "Indian Couple Having an Argument" were reprinted in the chapbook *From a White Woman's Journal*, Water Mark Press, 1985.

"Love Affair in a Small Town," "*Bildungsgedicht*," "Another Look at 'Albion on the Rock': Plate 38 of Blake's *Milton*," and "Last Dream in Perú" were reprinted in the chapbook *Carolyne Wright: Greatest Hits 1975-2001*, Pudding House Publications (invitational series #153), 2001.

"The Custody of the Eyes," as title poem of a related series, received the Pablo Neruda Prize from Nimrod (selected by Mark Strand).

"Darwin's House at Downe (Closed Fridays)" received the Cecil Hemley Memorial Award from the Poetry Society of America (selected by Donald Hall); and Third Prize in the first annual Ann Stanford Poetry Prize from the University of Southern California (selected by Bill Matthews).

"Studies with Miss Bishop" received three nominations for a Pushcart Prize, 2003.

I also thank the Bread Loaf Writers Conference, the Mary Ingraham Bunting Institute of Radcliffe College, the Creative Artists Public Service (CAPS) Program of New York State, the Fine Arts Work Center in Provincetown, the National Endowment for the Humanities, the Port Townsend Writers Conference, the Seattle Arts Commission, Seattle University, Syracuse

University, the Summer Literary Seminars—Saint Petersburg (Russia), the Vermont College Postgraduate Writers' Conference, the Washington Poets Association, and the Corporation of Yaddo for fellowships and awards that provided support while I was completing this book.

For their reading of and suggestions for poems in this manuscript, I am grateful to Christopher Bursk, Emily Hiestand, Ha Jin, James McKean, Stephanie Painter, Betsy Sholl, Leslie Ullman, and Deborah Woodard. Special thanks to Roger Weingarten for his encouragement, and to Ethelbert for a change of titles.

Carolyne Wright has published eight books and chapbooks of poetry, a collection of essays, and three volumes of poetry translated from Bengali and Spanish. Her previous collection, *Seasons of Mangoes and Brainfire* (Eastern Washington University Press/ Lynx House Books), won the Blue Lynx Prize and the American Book Award from the Before Columbus Foundation. Wright's investigative memoir of her experiences in Chile on a Fulbright Study Grant during the presidency of Salvador Allende, *The Road to Isla Negra*, received the PEN/Jerard Fund Award and the Crossing Boundaries Award from *International Quarterly*. Wright spent four years on Indo-U.S. Subcommission and Fulbright Senior Research fellowships in Calcutta and Dhaka, Bangladesh, collecting and translating the work of Bengali women poets and writers for an anthology in progress, *A Bouquet of Roses on the Burning Ground*, which received a Witter Bynner Foundation Grant and an NEA Fellowship in Translation, as well as a Fellowship from the Bunting Institute of Radcliffe College. A graduate of Seattle University's Humanities Honors Program with masters and doctorate in English and Creative Writing from Syracuse University, Wright has received awards from the Poetry Society of America, Seattle Arts Commission, and the New York State Council on the Arts, and she has been a Writing Fellow at the Fine Arts Work Center in Provincetown, Vermont Studio Center, and Yaddo. A visiting professor at colleges, universities and writers' conferences throughout the U.S., Wright has returned to her native Seattle, where she serves on the faculty of the Whidbey Writers Workshop MFA Program, and on the Board of Directors of the Association of Writers and Writing Programs (AWP).